Original title:
The Succulent Garden

Copyright © 2025 Creative Arts Management OÜ
All rights reserved.

Author: Theodore Sinclair
ISBN HARDBACK: 978-1-80581-862-5
ISBN PAPERBACK: 978-1-80581-389-7
ISBN EBOOK: 978-1-80581-862-5

## Resilient Beauty

Oh, the plants that laugh at drought,
Holding water like a stout.
They poke and prowl with cheeky flair,
In the sun, they strut without a care.

With leaves like shields and colors bright,
They joke with rocks, it's quite the sight.
When others wilt, they stand up tall,
In this garden, they have a ball.

## **Serenity's Palette**

Green and pink, a lively crew,
Dancing under skies of blue.
In the breeze, they hum a tune,
As squirrels plot mischief by the moon.

Each flower boasts a quirky face,
In this colorful, joyful place.
They giggle softly, sipping sun,
In their stillness, life's just fun.

## Spiky Gemstones

Look at them, those prickly pears,
In a world where no one cares.
They sparkle bright, like little gems,
While avoiding pesky, hungry hems.

Cacti wear their spines with pride,
A prickly hug, or so they bide.
Under the sun, they're such a tease,
Who knew plants could be such fleas?

## Radiance in the Soil

Beneath the earth, it's quite a show,
With roots that wiggle to and fro.
They tickle worms and play charades,
In the dark, they form parades.

These hidden gems, they plot and scheme,
Growing tall, they chase a dream.
With laughter spilled across the ground,
In their embrace, joy knows no bounds.

## Guardians of the Grit

In pots so stout, they stand with pride,
Thorns with charm, they do not hide.
Water them little, give them a laugh,
They'll thrive on sunshine, not the staff!

Their colors pop with joyous flair,
Watch out, they might just steal a chair!
With wrinkled leaves and cheeky grins,
Crowd there, you'll find who truly wins.

## Tenderness in Toughness

Some wear armor, others are meek,
A cactus softens with a little cheek.
When friends come round for tea and treats,
Pies and warmth, no one concedes!

Between the spines, you hear a joke,
A giggle sprouts from each prickly poke.
Laughter blooms where harshness reigns,
Soft-hearted jokes break all the chains.

## A Patch of Daring Delight

Come feast your eyes on greens so bold,
Where giggles sprout and tales are told.
 Each leaf a story, a twist, a spin,
 Oh, what a ruckus, let's dive in!

A mishap here, a tumble there,
A garden that's full of silly flair.
 Beware the wobbly pot brigade,
They dance around, and mischief's made!

## **Solace Amongst Succulents**

In this retreat where spines make peace,
Companions thrive, troubles cease.
Banter blooms in the soothing sun,
Who knew that pricks could be such fun?

They gather round for stories shared,
With every poke, they know you cared.
In playful jests, they root for life,
A thriving patch free from strife.

## Blossoms of Starlight

In a land where cacti dance,
With twinkling feet and a silly glance,
They wear their hats made out of sun,
Playing peek-a-boo, oh what fun!

Swaying to the tunes of night,
They gather round in soft moonlight,
With jokes that make the lizards laugh,
Their prickly wit a delightful craft!

## Lush Parables

Once a sage was found in green,
With a cactus cat, a silly scene,
He claimed the soil spoke in rhymes,
But all it said were silly chimes!

The herbs would chuckle, leaves would shake,
At tales of bugs that tried to bake,
In pots of dirt and sunny rays,
Who knew plants had such funny ways!

## Heart of the Drought

When water's scarce in the bright sun,
The succulents plot, oh what fun!
They toss a party, drinks in hand,
With air plants twirling across the sand!

A barrel cactus brings snacks, so sweet,
While jaded leaves tap their tiny feet,
In parched lands where laughter flows,
It's the quirkiest garden that ever grows!

## Petals in the Wind

The petals flung upon a breeze,
Swirling softly with giggling tease,
They dance like kids who lost their shoes,
In joyful chaos, the garden grew!

A sunflower cracked a corny joke,
While pollen floated, oh what a hoax,
The bees buzzed back with chuckles galore,
In this bright patch, there's always more!

## A Tapestry of Thorns

In a patch of green, oh what a sight,
A cactus wears a tutu, ready for the night.
It dances with glee, but pricks with a smile,
Leaving puzzled gardeners stuck in denial.

Behold the aloe, looking quite slick,
Boasting of beauty with a spiky trick.
It whispers sweet secrets, all slimy and nice,
While each little thorn says, 'Don't come too close, slice!'

## **Warmth Beneath the Surface**

Underneath the sun, a lizard will lounge,
Basking on blooms where his friends like to hound.
He giggles at petals, all flopping about,
While bees buzz around, in chaos, no doubt.

With soil on their heads, the worms have a ball,
Throwing a party beneath roots so tall.
They dig and they dance, making quite the scene,
Creating a ruckus in their underground glean.

## **Echoes of Green**

A fuchsia mess shines, with colors so bold,
While cacti just grumble, feeling too cold.
'We love to be prickly!' they yell in despair,
'But how can we dance when we're stuck in mid-air?'

The greens have a laugh, a hearty good cheer,
'Come join our conga, there's nothing to fear!'
With thorns as their partners, they twirl all around,
Creating a circus right up from the ground.

**Prickly Embrace**

In this wild patch where chaos reigns,
Every plant tells a tale of joyous pains.
A literal hug from a spiny sweet friend,
Leaves us laughing though our patience can bend.

'Why are you so prickly?' a flower may ask,
'I'm guarding my heart, it's a thorny old task!'
With friendship like this, who needs soft and sweet?
Let's embrace our oddities - life is a treat!

## Oasis of Resilience

In a patch of green, they stand proud,
With leaves that wave like a quirky crowd.
Watering them feels like a dance,
They drink up my laughter, oh what a chance!

Their roots are tangled, but that's just fine,
Each one of them tells a joke or a line.
They giggle when the sun shines bright,
Sipping sunlight, what a delightful sight!

## Colors Beneath the Sun

Colors burst forth in a playful spree,
Greens and blues, shouting, 'Look at me!'
Petals blush like they just told a joke,
The sun winks back, oh, what a poke!

Orange and pink, they're in a debate,
Who's the brightest? Oh, it's a fate!
Each bloom a character, full of flair,
In this vibrant show, it's quite the affair!

## Thorns Wrapped in Softness

Thorns that sometimes prick a finger,
But oh, the blooms make my heart linger.
Wrapped in softness, an ironic twist,
Nature's joke, I can't resist!

With guards like knights, they stand with pride,
A prickly party, come join the ride!
Laugh at the danger, with a grin so wide,
In this oddball garden, I take my stride!

## Tales from the Verdant Sanctuary

Whispers of stories in the leafy maze,
Every corner holds a quirky gaze.
When the breeze plays with the leaves' tune,
You might hear laughter from a friendly prune!

Gather 'round, let the tales unfold,
Of mischief and mirth, bold tales told.
With roots deep in laughter, they play and sway,
In this green realm, we frolic all day!

## Dreams Among Spines

In a world where thorns abound,
Cacti dance with grace unbound.
They wave their arms, oh so divine,
While others cringe at every spine.

Succulents giggle in the sun,
Cactus jokes are just plain fun.
They toast to life, the driest cheer,
'Water? Nah, we've got this here!'

A tumbleweed rolls by with flair,
Saying life's a joke, don't you dare.
The prickly ones, so full of glee,
Make us laugh, oh yes, indeed.

So raise a glass of sandy grit,
For goofy greens that never quit.
In this garden, joy aligns,
Among the spines, we craft our signs.

## Harmony of Resistance

In a patch where the sun beats bold,
Plants stand proud, defying the cold.
With leaves like shields and smiles so wide,
They jest about how they won't hide.

A prickly pear sings a tune,
Under the watchful eye of the moon.
"Bring on the drought, we'll still survive,
With jokes so good, we're extra alive!"

Laughter bubbles from roots below,
While aloe plays the wise old show.
"Water? What's that?" it gently chides,
As laughter dances through these sides.

In harmony, they stand so tall,
With puns that brighten through it all.
In this realm, resistance is bliss,
With each spiked friend, we share a kiss.

## Oasis of Tranquility

In this space where humor thrives,
The verdant jokes bring us alive.
A lizard laughs, a sunbeam glints,
In the spots where no one squints.

Cacti bloom with quirky charm,
Offering hugs without the harm.
"Who needs water when you've got wit?
Join our dance, it's gonna be lit!"

A gentle breeze shakes the branches,
While succulents share their silly chances.
"What's the rush?" a jade plant quips,
"Just savor life on these juicy trips!"

In this haven, we find delight,
Where laughter echoes day and night.
An oasis crafted from glee,
Come join us here, carefree and free!

## The Art of Water Wisdom

In a land where rainbows rarely meet,
Plants have mastered the art of heat.
With sassy pricks and giggly roots,
Creating joy in their green suits.

"Hydration? Please, we're just fine,"
Says the agave with a cheeky line.
"We thrive on sun and quirky tales,
With laughter a ship that never fails!"

A jade plant whispers sweet advice,
"Make use of sun, don't think twice.
When troubles come, just grin and nod,
Laugh it off, give the world a prod."

So here we are, in jest we bask,
For wisdom shines behind every mask.
With each plant, a story spins,
In this mighty dance where joy begins.

## **Resilience Wrapped in Beauty**

In a patch where cacti dance,
They wear their spikes with pride and glee.
A laughing lizard steals a glance,
And wonders how they pee with those, you see?

The aloe waves as if to say,
"I'd like a drink, but not too much!"
It keeps it cool throughout the day,
While succulents pretend they're such a touch.

The jade plant counts its lucky stars,
While friends debate whose leaves are best.
With pockets full of prickly spars,
They laugh and claim to outshine the rest.

As blooms erupt, a chuckle's found,
For humor hides in every leaf.
In this patch, joy is unbound,
A garden full of bliss, no grief!

## Echoing the Earth's Embrace.

In the soil, a secret's sown,
A toadstool cracks a goofy grin.
It says, "I'm happy all alone,
But a water droplet's where I'll win!"

The earthworms wiggle to the beat,
While daisies sway in time with joy.
Who needs a friend when food's a treat?
Yet, they all still act like a buoy.

A beetle rolls a pebble big,
He thinks he's Atlas, strong and grand.
But oh, he slips—a little jig,
Now covered in dirt, just like he planned.

With each bloom, a laugh escapes,
For life here's silly, lush, and free.
Where nature thrives, and joy reshapes,
The punchlines grow with every leaf.

## Verdant Whispers

Leaves are gossiping, oh so sly,
"Did you see that bloom? Quite the sight!"
They chuckle as the bees buzz by,
Whispering tales of their flight.

A tiny sprout, he's green and bold,
Claims he can grow taller than the sun.
The older plants just roll their gold,
And laugh, for he's a tiny one!

Amongst the thorns, there's always fun,
A wacky seedling makes a plan.
To dress in petals, be the one,
To steal the show, a flowered man!

In this patch, with humor spread,
Bright colors dance, it's all a game.
Life's a joke, just laugh instead,
For growth and giggles, just the same!

## **Oasis of Color**

A rainbow's spill upon the ground,
Where colors burst and laughter's spry.
The daisies hum a silly sound,
They flirt with breeze as clouds go by.

The ferns in frills adopt a sway,
Pretending they're a dance parade.
While snails in line just take the day,
And claim their slow, unhurried trade.

Potted pals exchange a wink,
While chirping birds pipe up with tunes.
They share a secret with a drink,
And plot to grow some bigger prunes.

Amidst laughter, flowers bloom bright,
Each petal holds a joke or two.
In this space of sheer delight,
Color and joy just bloom anew!

## **Prickly Paradise**

In a land where cacti sway,
They laugh and dance, oh what a play.
With pointy hats and painted shoes,
These plants tell jokes, they never lose.

A spiky chef with mighty flair,
Whips up dishes with DIY hair.
He serves some salsa in a bowl,
But watch your step, or you'll lose a sole.

A beetle rides a prickly beast,
In this party, laughter won't cease.
They spike the punch, or so they claim,
But who would dare to share the blame?

So if you stroll through this delight,
Just mind your back and hold on tight.
With every turn, be warned, oh dear,
The laughs may sting, but it's all in cheer.

## A Tangle of Green

In a jungle of green, they play hide and seek,
With leafy friends, every day of the week.
A lizard's on roller skates, oh what a sight,
He twirls and spins, full of pure delight.

The aloe's got a secret, oh what will it be?
She whispers to the agave, 'Let's climb a tree!'
But when they try to reach for the sky,
A hysterical tumble makes them both cry.

A hedgehog joins in, with his fuzzy attire,
Setting up a disco, sparking the fire.
The succulents shimmy with pots on their heads,
Dancing all night, ignoring their beds.

In this tangle of green, mayhem's always found,
With belly laughs echoing all around.
It's a festival of fun, a joyous scene,
In a place where being silly is evergreen.

## Soothing Drought

In a sun-baked realm, dry as can be,
Plants are giggling, feeling so free.
'Water's overrated,' they slyly boast,
As they sip on sunbeams, a liquid toast.

The saguaro struts, with arms open wide,
Singing, 'Join me, friends, let's take a ride!'
But when a raindrop falls, they let out a yelp,
'Quick! Hide! We're getting water, no time to help!'

They sip on cold breezes, avoiding the flood,
As the cloud comes racing, boosting the bud.
But really, who needs a shower or rain,
When they can just laugh and dance through the pain?

In this dry, funny land of sun and cheer,
Every thirsty plant has the same kind of fear.
With a wink and a grin, they sing out with glee,
'Let's just hope the drought is a part of our spree!'

## The Art of Thorns

With arms all akimbo and heads held high,
The formidable flora are ready to fly.
'We're not just prickly, we're actually cool!'
Said the nacho cheese cactus, full of fuel.

They put on a show, with thorns in display,
'Come closer,' they shout, 'you'll love our buffet!'
A bowl of sharp chips with spicy delight,
Beware of the bites that emerge from the night.

A wise old fern giggles, 'Here's my decree,
Thorns are just art, come try out our spree!'
They paint with sunshine, the colors so bright,
On all the green leaves, it's a marvelous sight.

So when you wander through this prickly show,
Remember to laugh and let your joy grow.
For in the heart of thorns, you'll surely find,
A quirky, funny world, one of a kind.

## **Whispers of Thorny Serenity**

In a patch of spiky cheer,
Plants whisper without fear.
Giggles come from inch and sting,
While the cactus starts to sing.

One wore a hat, sharp and bold,
Another said, "I'm not that cold!"
They play at being soft and cute,
But don't you dare to try and scoot.

## Lush Leaves in Dappled Light


Leaves are dancing, what a sight!
Shadows play in the pale light.
They twirl and swirl with glee and grace,
But watch your step, or you'll lose face!

A leap here, a stretch there,
Little blooms are full of flair.
"Look at us, we rule the day!"
Just try to stop us, we dare play.

## Blooming Against the Odds

In a world of harshness, here we grow,
Striving hard, putting on a show.
If you think we're just for looks,
Get ready for our prickly hooks!

The blooms insist they're quite a catch,
In nature's game, we're built to hatch.
"Soft and cuddly, you might have missed!
Take a step back, or you'll be kissed!"

**Prickles and Petals**

With prickles sharp, and colors bright,
We lead the garden in delight.
"Don't touch me, I'm not a toy!"
"Just one hug, and you'll enjoy!"

Petals laugh, a joy to see,
While spiky friends hold tightly,
Together we create this space,
To bring a smile to every face.

# Reflections of Green

In the pot, a cactus grins,
With spines like tiny pins.
Each leaf a shout, a cheerful boast,
"Who needs water? I'm the host!"

A jade plant wears a leafy tie,
Swishing leaves, oh my, oh my!
Succulents dance in a sunny sway,
"Grab your hats, it's playtime, hey!"

Behind the bloom, a dust bunny hides,
"Don't blame me! I'm shy!" it confides.
Together we laugh, in our oasis bright,
Chasing shadows, in fringed sunlight.

Greenery's fun, a comedy spree,
In every pot, a secret glee.
Join the antics, plant your grin,
In this garden, we all win!

## Vivid Dreams of Drought

In a land where rain goes to play,
A cactus dreams of a cloudy day.
"Don't let the sun steal my chance,
I want to twirl, I want to dance!"

A rosette whispers, "Let's scheme!
We'll throw a party—bring the cream!"
With nectar cups, the guests are here,
Each one's a buddy, never fear!

The air is dry, but spirits soar,
Laughter echoes—who could ask for more?
Sipping light from the crescent moon,
The night's our stage, let's all attune!

So raise your leaf, let's drink and toast,
To the thirst of life we love the most.
In vivid dreams, we find our way,
Join this drought, come out and play!

**Graces of the Cacti**

Oh cacti, such graceful spiky sights,
Waving to us with their prickly rights!
"Don't touch my hair, it's not a toy,
But I can be your pointy joy!"

A ball of fuzz bobs in the breeze,
"I'm not a dessert, but I'm quite a tease!"
With a wink and nod, it rolls around,
Scaring garden gnomes, let's leave them bound!

The noble aloe, so full of pride,
Swears it's the best in the plant world wide.
"Just ask my gel, I'm quite the deal,
Slather me on, and I'll make you heal!"

In this green parade, a humorous plot,
Each plant insists, "Don't forget me, hot!"
With every quip, they spark delight,
These graces of glee glow incandescently bright!

## The Colors of Resilience

In shades of pink and vibrant green,
These tough little warriors are quite the scene.
"Rain or shine, we're here to stay,
Watch us thrive, come what may!"

A golden barrel with a sunny glow,
Said, "I'm the beacon, come see my show!"
While jade shoots giggle, spreading cheer,
"Where's the water? We don't live in fear!"

With petals blooming, bright as a dream,
They gather 'round the sunlight's beam.
"Bring on the drought!" they lovingly cheer,
Our color is resilient, let it be clear!

In this garden, laughter won't cease,
These hearty greens share a smile of peace.
With every shade, they paint the way,
In glorious hues, let's dance and sway!

## A Dance of Shadows

Beneath the sun, the cacti sway,
They throw their shadows in a play.
With prickly arms, they dance around,
Like party guests that can't be found.

In the garden, lizards scoot,
Wearing sunglasses, looking cute.
With tiny shades upon their nose,
They strike a pose among the rose.

The chubby toad leaps with a grin,
To join the party, let's begin!
He bumps a bloom and takes a spin,
It's hard to tell who's lost or win.

As evening falls, the shadows grow,
With giggles from the plants below.
In silliness, the garden thrives,
With quirky vibes, the humor drives.

## Flora's Resilience

A cactus told a tale so grand,
Of sneaky winds upon the sand.
With thorns like armor shining bright,
In battles fought, it won the fight.

The daisies laugh, they bloom and tease,
Waving gently in a breeze.
With petal caps and silly hats,
"Oh look, we're cutting class!" they chat.

A stubborn weed, it wiggled free,
Challenging the rain and bee.
"Here I stand, a blooming clown,
With roots so deep, I wear a crown!"

Through storms and drought, they keep it light,
In colors bold, they shine so bright.
Nature's jesters, brave and bold,
In every corner, tales unfold.

**Nature's Jewel Tones**

In a garden filled with hues so bright,
The flowers giggle in morning light.
A violet winked at a golden rose,
"Hey there, friend! I've got a pose!"

The lilies join in with a sway,
"Watch us dance; we're on display!"
With colors clashing, all in fun,
Under the warmth of the big round sun.

The hummingbirds buzz, full of cheer,
"Who's the fairest, let's make this clear!"
Each bloom puffs up with a sly grin,
"Let the fabulous race begin!"

As evening falls, they hold a ball,
With petals swirling, one and all.
Their laughter echoing through the night,
In jewel tones, what a delight!

## Oasis of Serenity

In a calm spot, where laughter grows,
A turtle giggles, and the wind blows.
"Join the party!" the plants all sing,
With chessboard leaves, they start to swing.

The fish below, they flip and flop,
With swishing tails, they never stop.
"Who needs water guns for fun?
Catch us if you can! We're on the run!"

Bamboo sneezes with tidy grace,
"As if you'd ever win this race!"
A bounce and stretch, then flies away,
With gentle humor, they play all day.

As twilight lands, they settle down,
In whispers soft, no need to frown.
An oasis, full of laughter's charms,
In nature's arms, it's pure and warm.

## Harmony of the Hardy

In pots so round, with colors bright,
They wiggle and dance in morning light.
Cacti wear hats, it's quite a sight,
Dressed up for tea, oh what a delight!

Succulents gossip, their pearls on show,
Whispering tales of the garden glow.
With roots so deep, they steal the show,
While sunbathing, in rows they grow.

A parched joke here, a pun so dry,
They chuckle at rain clouds passing by.
Each leaf a punchline, oh me, oh my!
In their green jokes, the silliness is nigh!

With spines and smiles, they're never shy,
A hardy crew under the wide, blue sky.
In laughter's embrace, they sprout up high,
The garden's comedy, oh my, oh my!

## Sunlit Sanctuary

In a sunlit nook where laughter grows,
The sunbeams tickle, like playful toes.
A wily aloe, with wit that flows,
Cracks up the cosmos with its wise prose.

A potbellied jade with a comical stance,
Wobbles and giggles, it loves to dance.
With every breeze, it takes a chance,
To sway along in its leafy prance.

The bees all buzz, they want to hear,
The unruly tales of the garden dear.
With shenanigans shared, they persevere,
Creating a ruckus, a boisterous cheer!

As shadows stretch and day does close,
These plants know well how laughter grows.
In this haven where silliness flows,
The light-hearted spirits steal the show!

## The Resilient Bloom

A cheeky bloom in a cracked-up pot,
It stretches wide, ready or not.
With roots like anchors, it laughs a lot,
Surviving whatever the weather's got.

It wears a hat made of tin and dreams,
While sipping sunshine and sunny creams.
With petal punchlines and dazzling gleams,
Its humor bursts forth, or so it seems.

When rain does come, oh what a scene,
They pop out umbrellas, all bright and green.
In puddle-splash parties, they're quite the team,
Celebrating life with giggles and gleam.

With a wink and a grin, they flaunt their charms,
In this jolly garden, with all its farms.
Resilient giggles, the best of arms,
In nature's laughter, they work their balms!

# Secrets of the Drought-Defiant

In a parched patch with secrets untold,
These daring greens are brave and bold.
With spiky charm and stories old,
They laugh at drought; their humor is gold.

Gathering whispers from the sun's warm rays,
They trade jokes in their quirky ways.
Clapping their leaves in hilarious praise,
For every dry day, they craft clever plays.

The drama unfolds with every breeze,
As each spindly stalk bends with ease.
In this garden, smiles come to tease,
And humor flows freely like honeyed bees.

Secrets of joy in the arid scene,
Defiant and bold, like a playful queen.
With snickers and giggles, they're evergreen,
In this patch of laughter, a silly routine!

## Whimsical Watering

In a pot, a cactus grins,
With tiny arms, it waves and spins.
Plants demand a drink each day,
But soil steals sips and trots away.

A watering can with a frown,
Dances wildly, spills it down.
Each droplet lands, a splashy show,
Who knew plants loved a water glow?

A succulent whispers, 'This is fun!'
While neighbors laugh, they bask in sun.
In the circle of friends, they root,
Sipping sunshine, oh what a hoot!

Poking fun at thirsty leaves,
They giggle, dance, like playful thieves.
In this garden, joy abounds,
With every splash, laughter resounds.

## Flavors of the Arid

In the heat, the plants conspire,
One claims to taste like fried desire.
Another shouts, 'Try me with spice!'
'No thanks,' I say, 'You're just not nice.'

A rosette claims it's peachy keen,
While others argue, 'More like green!'
With flavors bold, they joke and tease,
'We're the snacks for hungry bees!'

Agave winks, 'I'm syrupy sweet,
Perfect for a breakfast treat!
Just grab a spoon, come take a bite,'
But all I want is a cup of light.

Cacti argue who's the best,
In their prickly little quest.
While I sip my drink nearby,
They flaunt their flavors, oh my, oh my!

## **Nature's Artistry**

In pots lined up like standing art,
Each plant has flair, a quirky part.
One's a painter, green and bold,
While others claim they're coins of gold.

With petals bright like comic strips,
Each leaf insists it's got the quips.
A sculptor's touch, they twist and turn,
As if they've come to watch and learn.

In this gallery of delight,
Prickly pears argue day and night.
'My form is best!' the agave shouts,
As all around, the laughter sprouts.

With nature's brush, they twist and twine,
Creating laughs like some fine wine.
Each little gem, a silly muse,
In this yard of artist hues.

## Spheres of Serenity

In a circle, the plants all stare,
With little worries, without a care.
They chat about the clouds above,
And wonder which will fit their love.

'Let's lounge today, feel the breeze,'
Says jolly jade, with such great ease.
'Pass the sunshine, don't leave me out!'
While others join in, laugh, and shout.

A potbellied friend starts to snore,
In this circle, oh, we want more.
With dreams of growth and sweet delight,
They share their hopes throughout the night.

The spheres of green, united, whole,
Filling gardens with laughter and soul.
In harmony, they cheer and sway,
A joyful crew, come join the play!

## Resilience in Bloom

In a pot so round and bright,
Lies a cactus, what a sight!
With needles sharp and grin so wide,
It's a prickly friend with plant pride.

Told a story to the rose,
"If it rains, I'll wear a hose!"
Both laughed hard, the sun did shine,
In this garden, all is fine!

A fern laughed at a tiny sprout,
"You'll be tall, there's never doubt!"
The sprout replied, a cheeky shake,
"Just wait and see the leap I'll make!"

Insects dance with leafy glee,
"Hey there buddy, come and see!"
In this fun-filled green locale,
Who knew growing could be so pal?

## Bounty of the Sun

Beneath the sun, the plants conspire,
Sipping rays like sweet satire.
A tiny leaf, with arms outstretched,
Said to the sun, "We're so well-matched!"

Oh, how the clover loves to laugh,
She tickles roots, oh what a gaff!
"Try using humor to survive,"
Said the sage, with a wise high five!

The daisies spin and faintly twirl,
"Is that a worm or just a swirl?"
Worm grinned wide, his face so sincere,
"Let's dig into this soil right here!"

A playful breeze joins in the fun,
Rustling leaves, oh what a run!
And as they sway, the laughter grows,
In this patch of life, joy overflows!

## Sun-drenched Whimsy

On a sunny day, the squads unite,
Cacti bear arms, ready for flight.
"Let's go cruising, rock the scene!"
They rolled and tumbled, a desert dream!

Bouncing pebbles share some jokes,
With sassy thorns that poke and poke.
"Who's the funniest plant of all?"
The aloe claimed, "I'm standing tall!"

Butterflies flutter with tiny sighs,
Reading leaves, oh those cruel lies!
"Who wore it best? That cactus green?"
"Not me," said one, "I'm just a bean."

The sun dips low, they cozy up,
Whispering tales while sipping cup.
With laughter strong, their roots embrace,
In this garden, joy finds its place!

## Intricate Succulents

With shapes like puzzles, stacked so neat,
These greens have got some funky beat.
A swirl of colors, a dizzy dance,
"Join us, come on, give it a chance!"

The leafy friends watched time unfold,
While trading secrets bold as gold.
"Does this bloom make me look fat?"
Said a plump little lad, all well fed and that!

Squished and smooshed in a sunny clump,
The laughter echoed with every bump.
"Who needs water when you've got style?"
Cried out one, with a cheeky smile!

Thus in this plot, a tale so grand,
Spreads like vines across the land.
As seasons change, they always thrive,
Bringing joy, and keeping life alive!

## Celestial Flora

In pots of dreams, they twirl with glee,
Those spiky plants love to dance with me.
They puff their cheeks, so round and grand,
While I just can't seem to understand.

With leaves like arms, they wave hello,
Each morning brings a leafy show.
They gossip softly, in whispers shy,
'Did you see the sun? Oh my, oh my!'

## Nature's Quiet Strength

A cactus wore a tiny hat,
Declaring proudly, 'I'm where it's at!'
With roots so deep, it takes a stand,
Against the winds, it's rather grand.

The succulents share a cheeky grin,
'We thrive on laughter and a little sin.'
In dry debates, they stake their claim,
'We're tough, we're bold, we're not so tame!'

## Harmony of Drought

A lizard passed, with a wink and a grin,
Said, 'In this dry land, we're all kin!'
'Grass may complain, and flowers may pout,
But we've got style; check us out!'

With wrinkled skin, they strut so proud,
In this arid place, they form a crowd.
'Who needs water when we have fun?
Our dry humor shines like the sun!'

## **Sun-Kissed Resilience**

Beneath the sun, they bask and play,
Chasing shadows through the day.
With wicked jokes on the breeze,
They laugh at storms with perfect ease.

"Fretting's no fun," a plant yelled loud,
"We're fierce and plucky, that's why we're proud!"
So cheers to those with grit so fine,
In this cheeky world, we always shine!

## Lush Embrace

In a plot where greens entwine,
Cacti wear capes of sunshine,
The agaves gossip wild tales,
While ferns dress in leafy veils.

Hiding bugs in their midst lay,
Frogs sing loudly, come what may,
Laughter erupts with each shake,
A garden dance, make no mistake!

Succulents twirl in breezy spin,
Claiming victory, let the fun begin!
Their spines aren't sharp, just a guise,
For squishy hugs and friendly cries.

Amidst the laugh, watch snails creep,
With secret plans they'd rather keep,
Slipping fast, they're quite the sight,
In this jungle of pure delight.

## Desert Blooms

In dry lands, blooms come alive,
They dance and sway, oh what a hive,
Chasing bees with laughter loud,
While prickly pears form a proud crowd.

With colors bright, they paint the view,
Yellow, pink, and shades of blue,
A cactus jumps, but with no grace,
"Look at me!" it shouts, in its place.

A lizard winks, a funny chap,
Sunning well, taking a nap,
While playing tag among the leaves,
With tricks and stunts, no one believes.

From sandy rocks, the flowers cheer,
In laughter, bring each other near,
For in this dry, yet vibrant land,
Funny frolics bloom, as planned.

## **Eden of Resilience**

Amidst the trials, colors shine,
Sturdy plants, such brave design,
Insects debate just how to thrive,
Making bets to stay alive.

With potting soil as their throne,
They root for fun, none alone,
"Let's grow taller!" one did shout,
And off they went to stretch about.

A tumbleweed joins the show,
Rolling in with all its glow,
While the aloe gives a sly grin,
Saying, "Let the games begin!"

Each leaf a story, bold and bright,
A comedy in morning light,
Together they forge their fate,
In this garden that can't wait.

# Nectar in Sunlight

Blooming with nectar sweet and rare,
Flowers chuckle, light as air,
Bees buzz by with comical grace,
Where sweetness drips from every place.

The sun pulls pranks, a playful tease,
Sunny beams tickle leaves with ease,
"Come dance, dear flora!" they all chant,
A lively ball, oh, what a plant!

Vines entwine, they sway and bend,
In joyous loops, they all pretend,
To be a hula dancer proud,
Shouting laughs that draw a crowd.

Oh, gather round, dear critters small,
Join the revels, one and all,
For in this vibrant world today,
Laughter blooms in nature's play.

# Tapestry of Life

In a patch of green, a cactus wears a hat,
Next to a lonesome fella, a chubby little sprat.
They play a game of tag with the sun's warm rays,
Chuckling as the garden dances in endless plays.

A rosette giggles at a passing bee,
And shouts, "Hey there, what do you want from me?"
The bee just buzzes with a joyful cheer,
"I'm here for the nectar, my friend, have no fear!"

The agave winks with a spiky grin,
While the hawthorn yells, "Let the games begin!"
They strut and sway like a crew of clowns,
Living their lives in their prickly crowns.

In this cheerful patch, life's a silly ride,
With laughter echoing in every side.
Each plant a character, each leaf a joke,
In the tapestry of life, happiness is bespoke.

## Sunlit Fables

The sun peeked in, cast a warm embrace,
As a golden flower flaunted its face.
A lizard retorted, "Why so full of glee?"
"You wouldn't understand, I'm as bright as can be!"

A plump jade plant wanted to dance,
But its stems were stiff, not the best for a prance.
So it jiggled a bit on its tiny little toes,
While the daisies laughed, striking silly poses.

A sly old tortoise watched from below,
Roaming the sunny paths, oh so slow.
"It's not about speed, but the fun you can have,
Taking your time, enjoy every lav!"

In this sun-soaked realm where laughter thrives,
The stories are many, the joy it derives.
Each plant and critter in a comic strife,
Creating a fable that's bursting with life.

## Hidden Oasis

In a secret nook where the wild things play,
A fern tells tales of its good ol' days.
The moss giggles softly, "Let's make a show,
Dance the night away, just watch me glow!"

A naughty little toad hopped into the mix,
With a croak so loud, it made the flower fix.
"Quit your booming, you ribbiting fool!
You'll start a dance-off at this leafy school!"

Every plant jostled, each creature swayed,
Plotting a caper, oh what a parade!
The palm tree chuckled, shaking its fronds,
As the stars turned on their twinkling wands.

In this hidden huddle, laughter is thick,
With a sprinkle of mischief, we all get a kick.
The oasis of humor, submerged in glee,
Where the secret's delight is forever carefree.

**Earthly Sculptures**

Nature's canvas stretched across the field,
With prickly hedgehogs, its wonders revealed.
Rocks whisper tales with a rumbling cheek,
As the soil chuckles, "I'm here for a peek!"

A cheeky little sprout peeked from the bed,
"Look at me grow, better than bread!"
While a crooked old stone grumbled with pride,
"Can't hold a candle to my rugged side!"

The wind played tricks, swaying the scene,
Switching the flowers in a capricious routine.
They twirled and twisted with a dazzling flair,
"A garden, a circus! Who needs a fair?"

In this earthly exhibit, humor grows strong,
With laughter as vibrant as a garden song.
Each plant stands proud, with stories to spin,
Creating a masterpiece where joy shall win.

## Gentle Giants of the Soil

In a realm where spines stand tall,
They whisper secrets, heed my call.
With patches of laughter, they jive and sway,
Plant princes in a soil ballet.

A cactus tried to tell a joke,
But somehow, it just went broke.
It pricked the puns and made me groan,
Yet somehow, it still felt like home.

With every poke and every grin,
These gentle giants let fun begin.
They wear their thorns like crowns of gold,
In this kingdom, humor will never grow old.

So if you find yourself in a spot,
Among these beings, I promise a lot.
Bring your chuckles, leave your frowns,
In this land, laughter always crowns.

## In the Embrace of Green

In a world that's snug and bright,
The greenery tickles with pure delight.
Poking fun with each gleaming leaf,
Even the roses try to be brief.

One plant told another, "Don't be so meek!"
But it broke into laughter and felt a bit weak.
With chlorophyll dreams and water come true,
They dance through the night; oh, how they grow!

The grass giggles under foot, so soft,
As petals sway 'neath the laughing loft.
Buds bubble up like soda cans,
These green pals have the best of plans!

So waltz with me in this leafy embrace,
Forget your troubles; leave not a trace.
In this joyful garden, let spirits soar,
With plant pals who will make you roar!

## **Dancers in the Desert Breeze**

In the dry land where the sun does shine,
Succulent friends sip water like fine wine.
They twirl and jiggle in playful glee,
Wearing their plumpness so carelessly.

A barrel cactus tried to join the fun,
But its stiff limbs couldn't quite run.
Instead, it wobbled, drawing chuckles around,
While shadows danced on sunbaked ground.

The yucca swayed with a comical flair,
Pretending to waltz without a care.
With each breeze, they shimmy and bend,
In this dance, there's laughter to send!

So let's all join in this sandy spree,
Where each little plant loves to be free.
With sun hats made of cactus spines,
The desert giggles with sparkling signs!

## Succulent Secrets Unfurled

Underneath a sunny sky so blue,
The plump leaves whisper secrets just for you.
With soft hues of green, they gossip and chime,
In this hidden world, humor's in its prime!

A jade plant chuckled, saying with pride,
"I'm not just a plant; I'm the whole joyride!"
It's the life of the party, so bold and spry,
With tricks up its sleeves, just give it a try.

The aloe waved, such a friendly chap,
Said, "Life is better when you take a nap!"
In a pot of cheer, under a sunlit beam,
These succulent wonders weave laughter's dream.

So let's dig deep where giggles abound,
In this garden, joy is always found.
With every glance, secrets unfold,
In a dance of plants, both brave and bold!

## Echoes of an Arid Haven

In a pot, a prickly pear, so proud,
Winks at a cactus, growing loud.
"I'm the king of this sandy realm!"
"Not if your spines are your only helm!"

Succulents giggle in the sun,
Making jokes about the dry run.
"Water me, just a little drop!"
"Careful now, you'll make me pop!"

A hummingbird's sip, that's the game,
Buzzing around, calling names.
"Let's party hard, with minimal rain!"
"Just don't invite the garden bane!"

In pots they dance, a wild show,
Jokes and jabs, oh what a glow!
Life's a jest in this desolate place,
With thorns and laughs, it's a funny space!

## **Nectar in the Nooks**

In crevices deep, where shadows loom,
Tiny blooms make the best of gloom.
"I'm sweeter than candy, come take a taste!"
"Just watch for the bees, they'll make haste!"

A lizard glides, in search of cheer,
"In this dry land, we persevere!"
"Got sunburned again, how tricky!"
"Don't fret, it's just a bit sticky!"

Rocky soils cradle giggles and glee,
With lopsided stems in a sunlit spree.
"Who said we can't have a little fun?"
"Just remember, hide when clouds run!"

They sip on sunshine and share the day,
In quirky corners, they laugh and play.
No need for water to wash away frowns,
In this funny nook, joy never drowns!

## Radiance in the Rough

When life gets tough and the sun is mean,
The spindly stalks put on a scene.
"We shine the brightest in the heat!"
"Let's outdo each other in this feat!"

A flower blushes in vibrant hue,
"Look at me! What do you do?"
"I'm home to the critters, and I stand tall!"
"Just don't give them a spiny ball!"

Barrels roll and giggles burst,
In this patch, it's humor we thirst.
"Forget the drought, let's make a joke!"
"Just don't blame me if your stems croak!"

With smiles etched in the desert dust,
Friendships grow strong, bloom is a must.
Amidst the rough, they twinkle bright,
Laughter sparkles in each sunlit sight!

## Cacti Chronicles

Once upon a time, in sandy skies,
A gang of cacti shared silly lies.
"I'm the tallest in this bright parade!"
"You mean the tallest that can't get laid!"

A tortoise trotted with tales to tell,
"You think you're cool? I know you well!"
"Your spines, my friend, look a bit grim!"
"But when it rains, I'll outshine him!"

In sunbaked lands, their stories grow,
With humor woven in every row.
"Let's have a feast with minimal sprouts!"
"Just bring the sun and killer clouts!"

As twilight dances on prickled greens,
The laughter echoes in leafy scenes.
In the chronicles of this merry crew,
With spines and smiles, they thrive anew!

www.ingramcontent.com/pod-product-compliance
Lightning Source LLC
Chambersburg PA
CBHW070334120526
44590CB00017B/2875